FIRST STEPS IN ORIGAMI

Origami Animals

Belinda Webster

I0808716

PowerKiDS press

Published in 2020 by **The Rosen Publishing Group, Inc.**
29 East 21st Street, New York, NY 10010

Cataloging-in-Publication Data

Names: Webster, Belinda.
Title: Origami animals / Belinda Webster.
Description: New York : PowerKids Press, 2020. | Series: First steps in origami | Includes glossary and index.
Identifiers: ISBN 9781725314887 (pbk.) | ISBN 9781725314900 (library bound) | ISBN 9781725314894 (6 pack)
Subjects: LCSH: Origami--Juvenile literature. | Animals in art--Juvenile literature.
Classification: LCC TT872.5 B437 2020 | DDC 736'.982--dc23

Copyright © Arcturus Holdings Ltd, 2020

All rights reserved. No part of this book may be reproduced in any form without permission in writing from the publisher, except by a reviewer.

Manufactured in the United States of America

CPSIA Compliance Information: Batch CSPK20: For Further Information contact Rosen Publishing, New York, New York at 1-800-237-9932.

CONTENTS

What Is Origami? 4

Puppy 6

Elephant..10

Crab..16

Rabbit 20

Glossary and Index..................................24

WHAT IS ORIGAMI?

Origami is the craft of paper folding, invented in Japan hundreds of years ago. The word "origami" means "folded paper" in Japanese.

Origami paper is thin but strong, so it can be folded many times.

It is square and is usually white on one side.

You could use ordinary scrap paper instead of origami paper, but make sure it's not too thick.

BASIC FOLDS

To follow the steps in this book, there are three basic folds you need to learn.

VALLEY FOLD

To make a valley fold, fold the paper up on itself so that the crease is at the bottom, like a valley. A valley fold will be shown by a dashed line, like this.

MOUNTAIN FOLD

To make a mountain fold, fold the paper the other way, away from you. You want the crease to point up, like the peak of a mountain. We use a dotted line to show a mountain fold.

STEP FOLD

A step fold is a mountain fold and a valley fold next to each other.

1 First, make a valley fold by folding the paper up on itself so the crease is at the bottom.

2 Now unfold.

3 Next, make a mountain fold above the valley fold you have just made.

4 Push the mountain fold over the valley fold and press it flat. You now have a step fold.

KEY

- - - - - Valley fold

.... Mountain fold

Step fold

Direction to move paper

PUSH Direction to push (or pull, etc.)

PUPPY

Here's a cute origami puppy, just for you. Once finished, you could create a whole doggy family by following the same steps on different sizes of paper.

1 Start with the paper like this. Valley fold it in half from left to right, then unfold.

2 Valley fold the left corner to meet the middle crease.

3 Do the same on the other side.

4 Rotate the paper so it looks like this. Then turn over the paper.

5 Mountain fold the paper in half, so that the top section goes behind the bottom section.

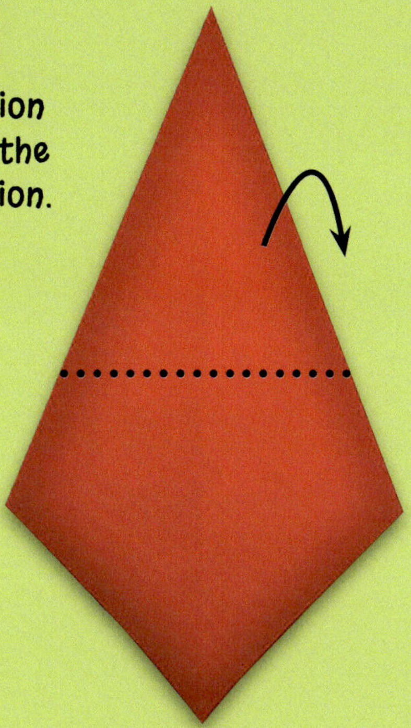

6 The paper should now look like this. Unfold.

7 Make a valley fold just below the crease you just made. This will make a step fold. Turn over the paper.

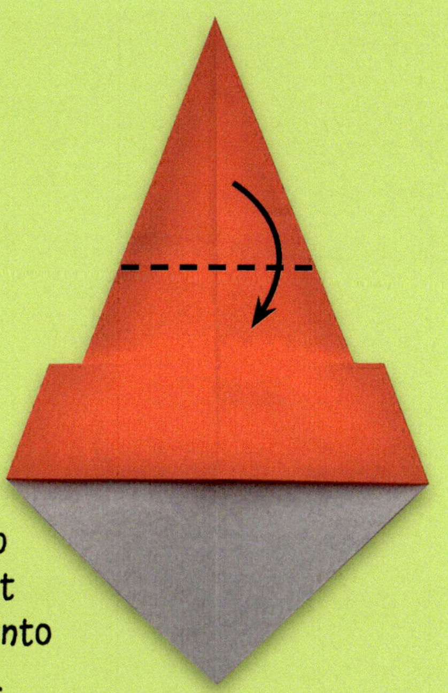

8 Valley fold the top down, so the point slightly overlaps into the white section.

9 Valley fold the bottom point up, so it slightly overlaps the tip of the point you just folded down. Tuck it under the point.

10 Valley fold the top section up and the bottom section down to create two step folds.

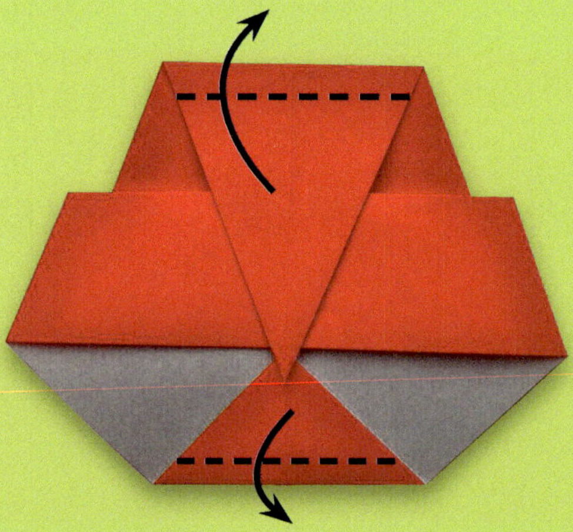

11 Valley fold the top point down as shown.

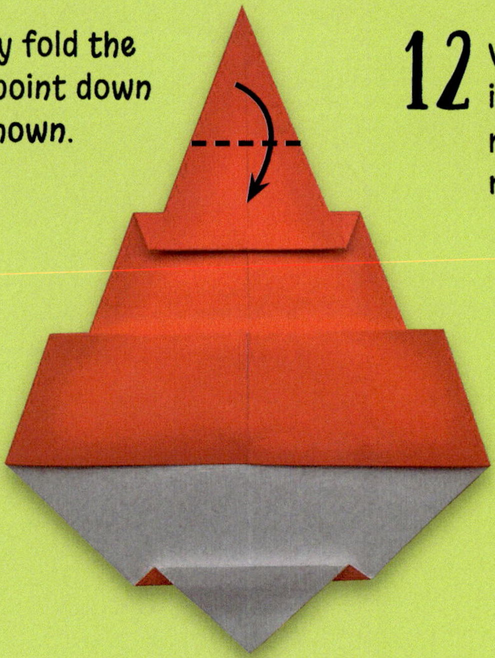

12 Valley fold the paper in half along the middle crease from right to left.

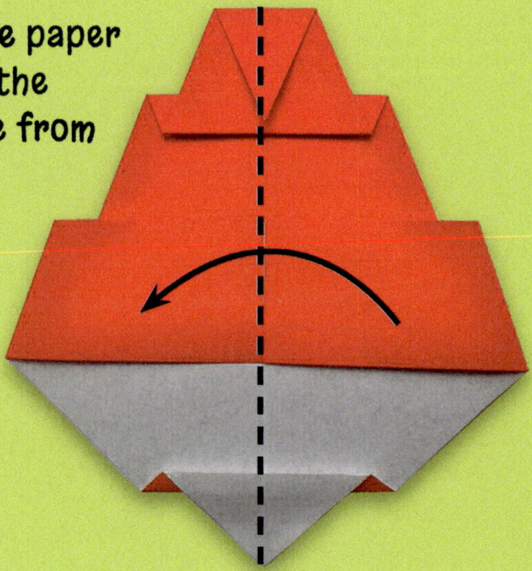

13 Rotate the paper to the left, so it looks like this. Valley fold as shown and crease well. Unfold, then gently push down on the puppy's nose, so the paper opens out at the front.

14 As you push down, the paper folds back to reveal the puppy's white feet. Press the leg flaps all the way back, flat on the puppy's body.

15 Stand up your origami model. You now have a perfectly cute puppy playmate!

DRAW SOME EYES, FRECKLES, AND A LITTLE BLACK NOSE TO COMPLETE YOUR PUPPY.

ELEPHANT

Elephants are the largest animals on land. Your paper model will be much smaller!

1 Place your paper white side up, like this. Valley fold it in half from right to left, then unfold.

2 Valley fold as shown, about a quarter of the way along the bottom left edge.

3 Do the same on the right side.

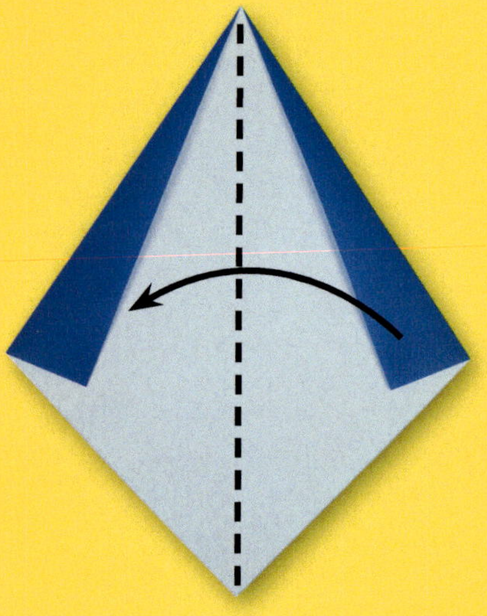

4 Valley fold the paper in half from right to left.

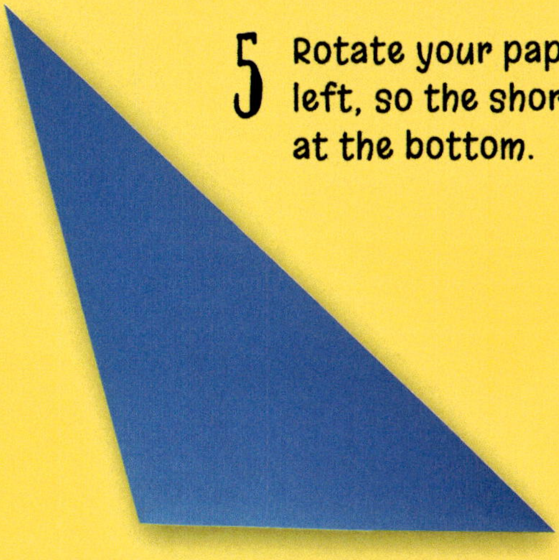

5 Rotate your paper to the left, so the short edge is at the bottom.

6 Valley fold the top left point over to the right, like this.

7 Open out the top pocket you created in step 6.

8 As you open out the pocket, push the top point down and flatten the paper.

9 Your paper should look like this. On the top piece only, make two small cuts along the solid lines shown. Mountain fold the paper behind on either side.

10 Make one mountain fold, followed by a valley fold. Then make another mountain fold, followed by a valley fold. These two step folds will create the elephant's trunk.

11 Your paper should look like this. Flatten the folds.

12 Make a mountain fold, followed by a valley fold, to create a step fold on the left-hand side, as shown. This will be one of the elephant's ears.

13 Repeat step 12 on the right-hand side, to create the other ear.

14 To make the elephant's tail, valley fold the right-hand point as shown. Then mountain fold it along the same crease. Unfold so it is flat again.

15 Create another valley fold, to the right of the fold you just made. Then mountain fold it back along the same crease, as you did in step 14.

16 Open out the end of the paper and tuck the tail inside the body along the crease you made in step 14. Flatten. Then fold it out along the crease made in step 15. Flatten. The tail should poke out, as shown.

17 To create your elephant's legs, use scissors to carefully cut out a small rectangle, like this.

DRAW EYES ON YOUR ELEPHANT'S HEAD AND SOME WRINKLES ON ITS TRUNK.

18 Gently pull the legs outward to make your elephant stand up on its own.

CRAB

Follow these instructions to create a friendly origami crab.

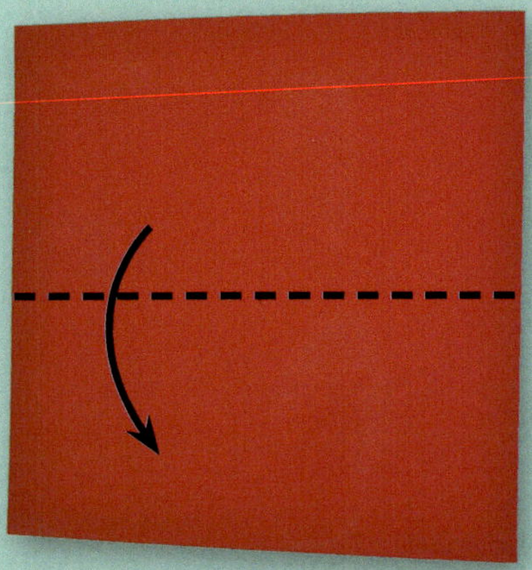

1 Place your paper white side down, like this. Valley fold it in half from top to bottom, then unfold.

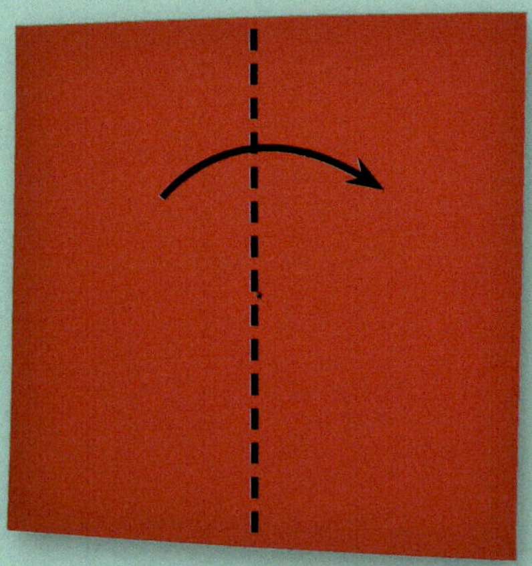

2 Valley fold it in half from left to right, then unfold. Turn over the paper.

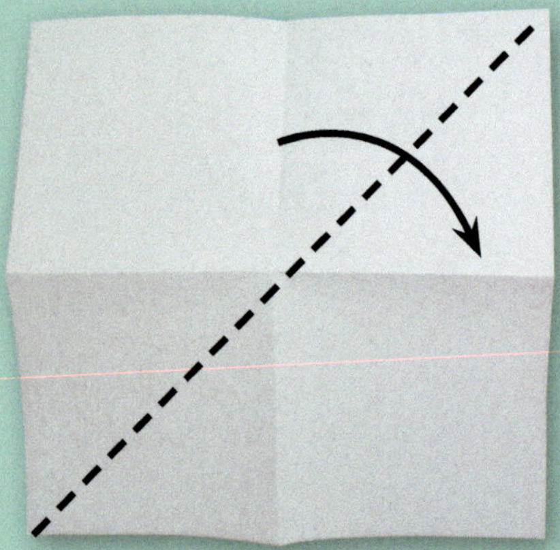

3 Valley fold diagonally, as shown. Unfold.

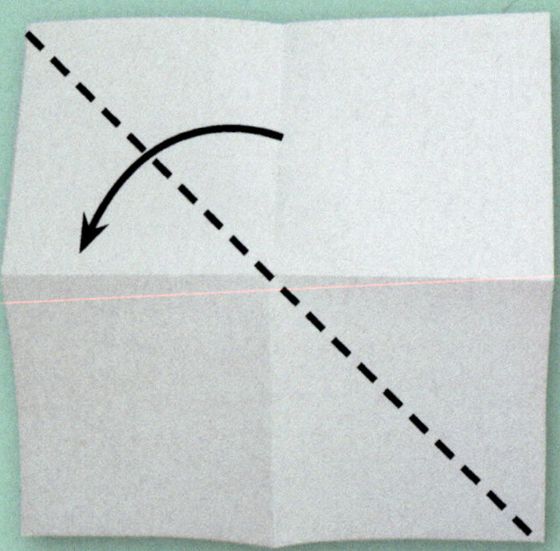

4 Now valley fold on the other diagonal, as shown. Unfold.

5 Push the two outer edges inward to meet each other.

6 The paper will fold down on itself to make a triangle shape. Press it down flat.

7 Your paper should look like this. Now rotate it, so that the central point faces down.

8 Mountain fold the top layer of the left corner, as shown, to form a claw.

9 Repeat step 8 on the other side to form another claw.

10 Mountain fold the top edge, as shown.

11 Your paper should look like this. Now turn it over.

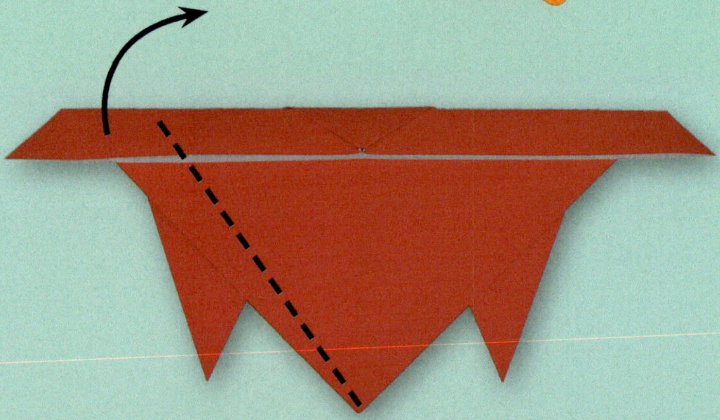

12 Valley fold the top layer on the left side, as shown, to create a pincer pointing upward.

13 Repeat step 12 on the right side.

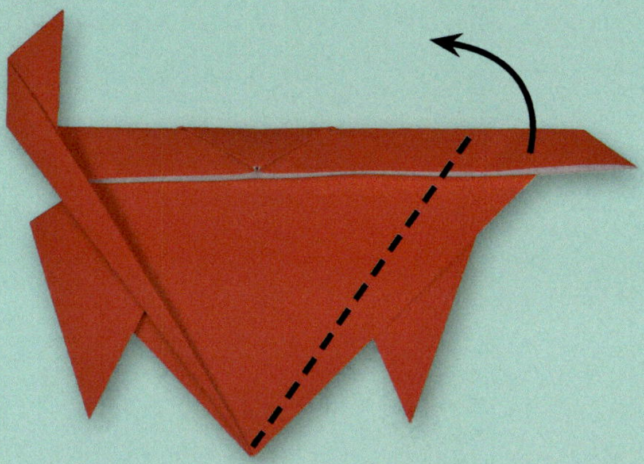

14 Valley fold the bottom point up, as shown.

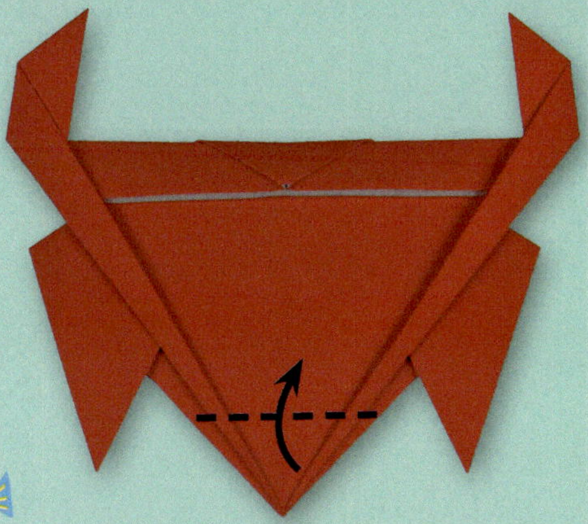

15 Your paper should look like this. Now turn it over. Your crab is ready to decorate.

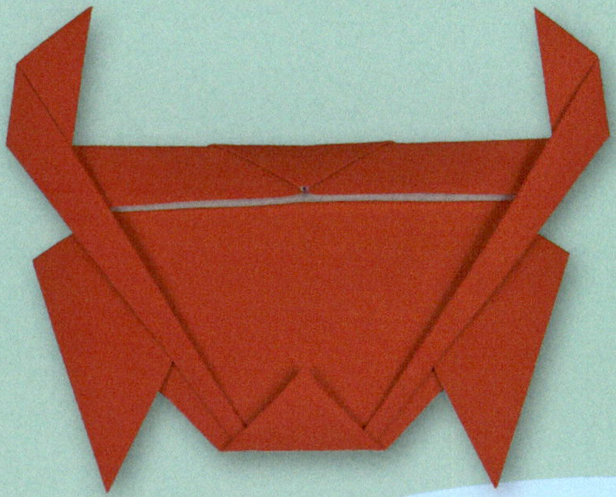

DRAW SOME EYES AND A SMILE TO BRING YOUR CRAB TO LIFE.

RABBIT

Make your own sweet little rabbit with superlong ears by following these steps.

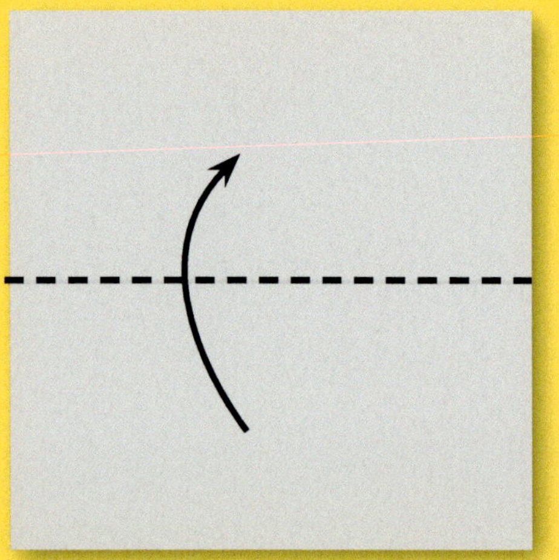

1 Place your paper white side up. Valley fold as shown, then unfold.

2 Valley fold the bottom section up to meet the middle crease.

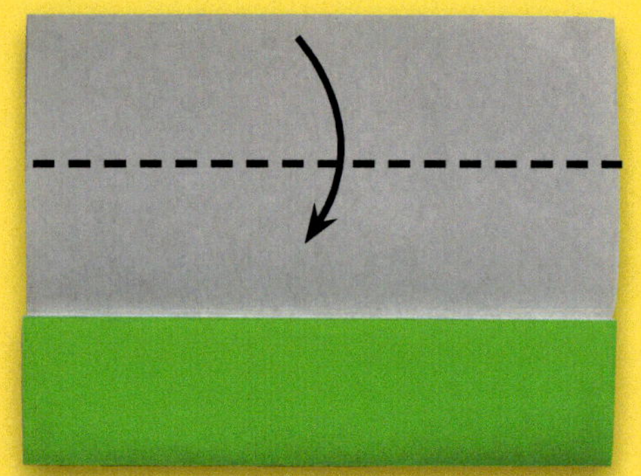

3 Do the same with the top section.

4 Valley fold the right corner down to meet the middle crease.

5 Valley fold the other corners in the same way.

6 Open out the corner folds.

7 Gently push the top right corner inside to create a flap along the creases, as shown. Flatten.

8 Do the same with the other three corners.

9 Turn over the paper. Valley fold the top layer of the left point and flatten down.

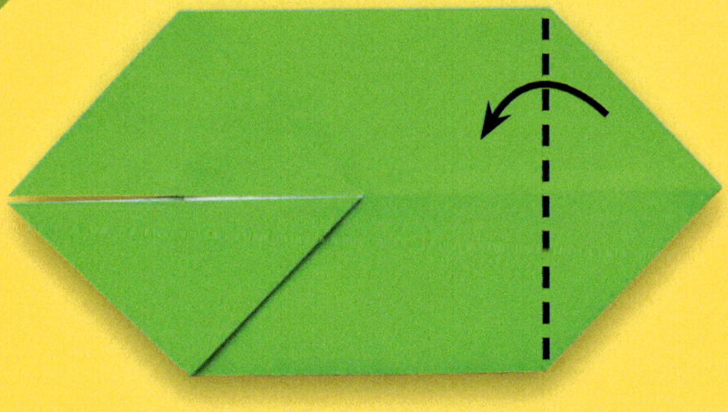

10 Do the same with the other side.

11 Your paper should now look like this.

12 Turn over the paper. Valley fold the top left corner to meet the middle crease, as shown.

13 Do the same with the bottom left corner.

14 To make the rabbit's ears, valley fold the left point, as shown. The flap underneath pops out to become the rabbit's nose.

15 Mountain fold the paper in half, along the middle crease.

16 Gently pull the ears up.

17 Press the paper as shown to flatten the head in position. Your paper should now look like this.

18 Valley fold the right point so the diagonal edge runs flat along the bottom of the model. Unfold.

19 Mountain fold along the same crease, then unfold. Open out the right end and fold the points inward, into the body. Flatten along the creases to make feet.

20 Valley fold along the line, as shown, then unfold. Mountain fold along the same crease, then unfold. Fold each point inward, into the body. Flatten to create the back of your rabbit.

21 Valley fold along the line, as shown, then unfold. Mountain fold along the same line, then unfold. Tuck the point in along the crease to create a nose.

GIVE YOUR RABBIT EYES, SOME WHISKERS, AND A CUTE NOSE.

22 Gently puff out the long ears to give them their shape. You now have an origami rabbit!

GLOSSARY

crease A line made by a fold.

diagonal A line in a sloping direction, from one corner to another.

mountain fold A fold where the crease points up at you, like a mountain.

pincers A crab's front claws.

rotate To turn in a circular movement.

step fold A fold that creates a zigzag, or step, in the paper.

valley fold A fold where the crease points away from you, like a valley.

INDEX

claws 17, 18
crab 16–19

ears 13, 20, 22, 23
elephant 10–15
eyes 9, 19

feet 9
folds
  mountain fold 4, 5
  step fold 5
  valley fold 4, 5

legs 14, 15

noses 9, 22, 23

paper 4
pincers 18
puppy 6–9

rabbit 20–23

tail 13
trunk 12